DISCOVER THROUGH CRAFT

RAINFORESTS

By Jillian Powell

W

FRANKLIN WATTS

LONDON • SYDNEY

First published in 2014 by Franklin Watts
Franklin Watts
338 Euston Road
London NW1 3BH

Franklin Watts Australia
Level 17/207 Kent Street
Sydney, NSW 2000

Series editor: Amy Stephenson
Series designer: Jeni Child
Crafts: Rita Storey
Craft photography: Tudor Photography
Picture researcher: Diana Morris

Picture credits:
Brandon Alaus/Shutterstock: 19b. Alfredo Amrquez/
Shutterstock: 12t. Stephane Bidouze/ Shutterstock:
27c. Blue Sky studio/Shutterstock: 4.Ryan N Bolton/
Shutterstock: 16cl. Nigel Dickenson/RHPL: 22t,
24b. Mark Edwards/RHPL: 24t. Katarina F: front
cover tr. guentermanaus/Shutterstock: 16bl. Janne
Hamalainen Shutterstock: 8b. Lisette van der
Hoom/Shutterstock: 26c. Robin Kay/Shutterstock:
1. Andrzej Kubik/Shutterstock: front cover c, 31t.
Oleksiy Mark/Shutterstock: 20. Andre Nantel/
Shutterstock: 14b. Piotr Naskrecki/Minden Pictures/
FLPA: 13. neelsky/Shutterstock: 6t. Pete Oxford/
Minden Pictures/FLPA: 16tr. Jesco von Puttkamer
RHPL: 21. V Raghard/Shutterstock: 28bl. Dr Morely
Read/Shutterstock: 10, 11t, 11c. Reuters/Corbis
Images: 26b. Arun Roisin/Shutterstock: 11b. A W
Seebaran/istockphoto: 14t. Still Pictures/RHPL:
22b. Kuttlevaserova Stuchelova/Shutterstock:
6b. Radka Tesarova/Shutterstock: 12b. taweesk
thiprod/Shutterstock: 6-7bg. Matt Tighmann/
Shutterstock: 32b. Voropaev Vasily Shutterstock:
8c. Wansford photo Shutterstock: 16cr. Christopher
Weilhs Dreamstime: 28br. worldwildlifewonders/
Shutterstock: 18. wong sze yuen/Shutterstock:
7. Kozoriz Yuriy/Shutterstock: 8t. Adrianne van
Zandbergen/FLPA: 19t.

Every attempt has been made to clear copyright.
Should there be any inadvertent omission please
apply to the publisher for rectification.

Dewey number: 333.7'5
HB ISBN: 978 1 4451 3101 6
Library eBook ISBN: 978 1 4451 3588 5

Printed in China

Franklin Watts is a division of Hachette
Children's Books, an Hachette UK company.
www.hachette.co.uk

CONTENTS

Words in **bold** can be found in the glossary on page 30.

Some of the projects in this book require scissors, paint and glue. We would recommend that children are supervised by a responsible adult when using these things.

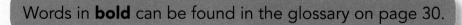

ABOUT RAINFORESTS

Every rainforest is different but they are all alike in some key ways.

Moist air hangs above the rainforest canopy.

What are rainforests?

Rainforests are forests of tall trees. They grow in warm or cool **climates** that have lots of rain all year round. Rainforest trees grow close together to form a **canopy** of leaves and branches that grow high above the ground. The tallest trees can reach heights of 60 metres. Rainforests are home to many kinds of plants and animals.

QUIZ TIME!

Which rainforest is the largest in the world?

a. the Amazon

b. the Congo

c. Daintree

Answer on page 32.

Where are they found?

There are two main kinds of rainforest. Tropical rainforests grow in the **tropics**, between the Tropic of Cancer and the Tropic of Capricorn, either side of the Earth's **Equator**. Here it stays warm and wet all year round. Some rainforests have more than 2.5 centimetres of rain nearly every day of the year. There are tropical rainforests in parts of Africa, Asia, Australia and Central and South America. **Temperate** rainforests grow along coasts in temperate zones, which lie between the tropics and the **polar** circles. The climate is cooler here but still mild and the air is often damp with mist, fog and rain. There are temperate rainforests in North America, Norway, Japan, New Zealand, South Australia, Ireland and the United Kingdom.

KEY:

Countries with the largest area of tropical rainforest:
1 Brazil
2 Democratic Republic of Congo
3 Peru
4 Indonesia
5 Colombia.

Largest area of temperate rainforest:
6 The Pacific coast, North America.

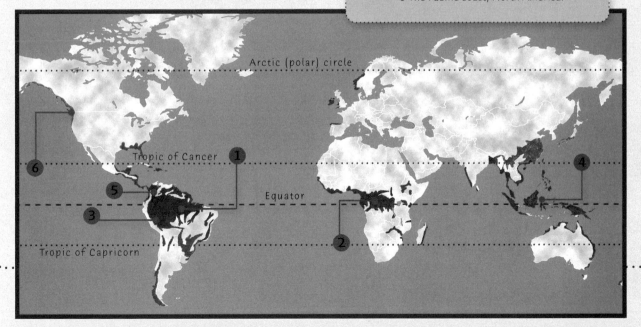

Arctic (polar) circle

Tropic of Cancer

Equator

Tropic of Capricorn

6
1
5
3
2
4

Quick FACTS

- Rainforests are forests with tall trees growing in either warm or cool climates.
- They have lots of rain all year round.
- They are home to many kinds of plants and animals.

WHY ARE RAINFORESTS IMPORTANT?

Rainforests are important because they protect the people and animals that live in them – and the whole planet.

Bengal tigers live in tropical rainforests in Asia.

A rich habitat

Rainforests provide a home for millions of plants and animals, including **mammals**, insects, birds and fish. Although they only cover about 6% of the Earth's surface, they contain half of all the plant and animal **species** on Earth. They are also home to **tribal** peoples who rely on the forest for shelter and food. Many of the medicines we use come from rainforest plants.

Climate

The trees and plants in rainforests soak up water through their roots, then release it as moisture through their leaves. The moisture helps to form rain clouds, which produce rainfall, both in the forest and around the world. Rainforests have also

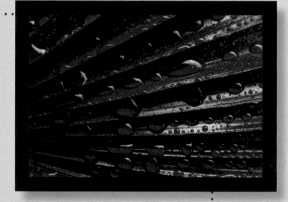

been called 'the lungs of the world' because they take in **carbon dioxide** from the **atmosphere** and produce **oxygen**, which all living things need to live and grow. Too much carbon dioxide can warm the Earth's atmosphere and cause **climate change** (p. 27) so rainforests help to keep our climate stable.

Many tropical trees have huge buttress roots that help stop soil erosion.

Soil and erosion

Tree roots help to keep soil in place, but when trees are cut down, the soil can wash away. This is called erosion. The roots of rainforest trees help stop rainwater flooding the land and stop soil from being washed away into rivers, where it can harm fish and other wildlife. The trees also help to keep soil and rocks in place on hillsides, where erosion can cause landslides. Landslides can be dangerous and threaten people, animals and their homes.

Quick FACTS

Rainforests:
• Produce rainfall around the world.
• Help keep the climate stable.
• Provide a home for people, plants and animals.
• Provide food and medicines.
• Help stop erosion and flooding.

? Why do you think the rainforest is such a rich **habitat** for plants and animals? Turn the page to find out.

The rainforest has three main habitats that are rich in animal and plant life.

The canopy

As rainforest trees grow tall their branches get squashed together. This forms a thick canopy where other plants grow and animals find food and shelter. Most rainforest animals and plants live up in the canopy – some will never touch the forest floor! Giant trees that grow even taller than the canopy form a top layer or 'overstory'.

Overstory

Canopy

Understory

Forest floor

HAVE A GO
Collect vegetable peelings and put them in a compost bin at home or at school. The peelings will slowly break down into a crumbly compost, which contains **nutrients to feed growing plants.**

The forest floor

The forest floor is under the cover of the canopy so it stays moist and shady. **Fungi**, mosses, insects and tiny living things called **microbes** (p. 11) live here. They help to **recycle** dead leaves and other animal and plant matter by breaking them down. Between the forest floor and the canopy is a layer called the 'understory' where smaller shrubs and plants grow.

Rivers and streams

The high rainfall feeds rivers, streams and creeks. Rainforests have some of the largest rivers in the world, like the River Amazon and the Congo River. They provide a home for fish, frogs and other animals and people use the rivers to move about by boat.

Make this

Rainforests are amazing habitats that create their own climate. Make your own mini rainforest in a bottle (or terrarium) to show how water is recycled by the rainforest plants.

Put your rainforest terrarium in a spot where it will get some light and shade. Look out for condensation on the sides of the bottle. This tells you that the water is being recycled. See how long your terrarium survives.

1 Ask an adult to cut the bottom 10 cm from a 2 litre plastic bottle. Fill it half full with stones.

2 Fill the bottom with soil, but leave a 2 cm gap at the top.

3 Plant two or three small tropical houseplants (evergreens with shiny leaves). Cover the top of the soil with moss.

4 Water the plants well, then add a plastic rainforest animal. Carefully place the top half of the bottle over the plants and the bottom part. Make sure the lid is secured on tightly with tape.

RAINFOREST TREES AND PLANTS

More than half of the world's plant species are found in rainforests.

An aerial view of part of the dense canopy of the Amazon rainforest.

Canopy trees

Most tropical rainforest trees tend to grow tall and straight. There are thousands of different types. There is so much competition for water and sunlight that only one seed in 10 million grows into a tree that will reach the canopy! Many tropical trees have broad, glossy leaves that rain drips off easily.

Temperate forests can have **deciduous** trees that lose their leaves, as well as **evergreens**, such as conifers, which have needles instead of leaves. Temperate and tropical forests provide us with many things we use, such as wood, fruit, rubber, medicines, chocolate and spices.

HAVE A GO
Try growing a tropical plant using mango, papaya or avocado seeds, after you've eaten the fruit. You can try sprouting seeds in water or plant them straight into moist compost.

Liana vines

Lianas are a type of climbing vine that have thick woody stems. They use roots or **tendrils** to attach themselves to trees and climb by winding themselves around the trunk or branches. When they reach the top of a tree, they can spread to other trees or wind around other lianas to form super-strong vines. Some can grow up to 900 metres long.

Smaller trees and plants

Palm trees, young saplings and shrubs grow in the understory, under the shade of the canopy. Sometimes a canopy tree comes crashing down. This lets in more light, which encourages more plants to grow.

Fungi and microbes

On the forest floor, where it is warm, damp and shady, fungi and tiny living things called microbes grow. They help break down dead plant or animal matter into nutrients. This process is called decomposition. Trees and plants take these nutrients up through their roots as food.

Many kinds of fungi grow on dead and rotting wood in the rainforest.

? **What other kinds of plants grow in the rainforest? Turn the page to find out.**

One tree can support lots of different types of epiphytes, such as these bromeliads.

Epiphytes

Epiphytes or 'air plants' grow on the branches and trunks of other trees and plants. They grow from seeds or **spores** carried by birds, animals or the wind. Mosses and ferns grow in temperate rainforests. Orchids, **bromeliads** and cacti grow in tropical rainforests. Some epiphytes, like the strangler fig, send long roots down to the ground to find nutrients. Strangler figs can become so big they take all the nutrients from the tree they are growing on and kill it!

Carnivorous plants

Some plants in the rainforest are **carnivorous**. This means they get food or nutrients from insects, spiders or even lizards and other small animals. Pitcher plants are shaped like tubes. They have a slippery surface so insects slide down into a sugary liquid inside. When the insect drowns and rots in the liquid, the plant soaks up the nutrients. Other plants have sticky hairs on their leaves to trap insects or they snap shut when an insect crawls inside.

QUIZ TIME!

How tall do you think most canopy trees grow in the rainforest?

a. **15 metres**

b. **45 metres**

c. **65 metres**

Answer on page 32.

These pitcher plants are sometimes called 'monkey cups' because monkeys have been known to drink from them!

Make this

Pitcher plants love the nutrients from a juicy insect or spider. Make these pitcher plants and play a game of fly tiddlywinks to see how many will be eaten! You can play against your friends and keep score.

Now you're ready to play the game. Keep score of how many you get into each pot. One point for pot 1, two points for pot 2 and three points for pot 3. The taller the pot the harder it is!

1 Cut cardboard tubes into three sizes – small, medium and large. Trim down the front half of each tube. Cover each tube in white paper. Tape in place and trim the paper to fit. Decorate to look like a pitcher plant (see main picture).

2 Cut three shapes, like the one shown (left), from stiff white paper. The bottom edge should be about 8 cm long. Decorate them as shown. Stick a red sticker onto each shape and give each one a number (1–3).

3 Use a pencil to curl over the top of each plant. Tape each top inside a tube.

4 Draw an insect on each of the tiddlywinks. You could draw a different type of insect for each player or use a different colour.

INSECTS AND OTHER MINIBEASTS

Lots of different kinds of insects and other minibeasts live in the rainforest.

Many minibeasts

Tropical rainforests are home to many kinds of minibeasts, such as butterflies, moths, beetles, stick insects, ants, spiders and worms. Insects are the largest group of animals that live there. Just one tree can be home to over 700 different species of insects! The rainforest provides water, shelter and food and it is warm all year round so some minibeasts are able to grow and **reproduce** all year. In temperate forests, many minibeasts live inside tree bark or on the forest floor, which is covered in dead plant and animal matter for them to feed on.

Goliath beetles live on the forest floor. They feed on rainforest fruits and climb up trees to feed on sugary tree sap.

Big and small

Rainforest insects range in size from tiny mosquitoes and ants you can hardly see, to giant beetles, spiders and some stick insects that can be 30 centimetres long. Some of the largest beetles on Earth, such as Titan and Goliath beetles, live in rainforests. They have powerful jaws for biting **prey** and sharp claws that help them to climb trees. There are also many different types and sizes of butterflies and moths. The largest grow to the size of small birds, with wingspans up to 30 centimetres across.

Beautiful tree nymph butterflies live in tropical rainforests.

HAVE A GO

Many minibeasts like living in dark, shady places like the forest floor. Make an insect habitat in the garden or at your school, using bits of wood, sticks, straw and clay flowerpots. Stack them closely together leaving small cracks for insects to hide in.

A leafcutter ant has sliced off a big piece of leaf with its powerful jaws.

Insect workers

Insects provide food for birds and other animals in the rainforest. They are also important because they help to clear the forest floor. Leafcutter ants carry leaves back to their nests. They chew up the leaves to make them into a sticky mass, which they store underground. A type of fungus grows on the chewed leaves, which the ants then eat.

? What defences do rainforest insects use to protect themselves against **predators**? Turn the page to find out.

Camouflage

Like other animals living in the rainforest, some insects use **camouflage** to hide themselves from predators. Stick insects can look like sticks or twigs. Leaf insects hang underneath trees to look like dead leaves. Some butterflies are hard to see because they look like dead leaves, or because they have wings you can see through, like the glasswing butterfly (right).

The moss mimic stick insect is camouflaged to look like the moss on a tree.

Defences

Many rainforest butterflies and moths are brightly coloured, with markings on their wings to stop predators eating them. Others have eye-like markings that make them look like animal faces. Some moth larvae look like scorpions, so predators avoid them because they think they might get stung. Caterpillars can be covered in stinging hairs or have bright patterns and colours that warn predators they may be poisonous. Bright reds, blues and yellows are common warning colours. Others use colours to look poisonous, even when they are not.

The bright colours of this caterpillar and the eye spots on the owl moth tell predators to stay away.

Quick FACTS

- Insects are the largest group of rainforest animals.
- Minibeasts can become food for birds and other animals.
- Insects also help to clear the forest floor by eating dead plants and animal matter.

Make this

Investigate the colours of rainforest butterflies. Use your research to inspire you to create this beautiful butterfly mobile.

1 Cut 10 cm circles and 10 cm squares of tissue paper. (You will need about eight of each in different colours.) Gently twist the middle of a paper circle and square. Fan out the tissue paper as shown.

2 To make one butterfly, tie a twisted circle below a twisted square with a long piece of thread. Repeat to make more butterflies.

3 Draw a spiral shape on a paper plate. Cut along the line you have drawn. Paint the plate on both sides and leave to dry.

4 Tie each butterfly to your spiral to make a mobile. Hang up the mobile.

You could hang your mobile in a window so the butterflies can flutter in the breeze.

OTHER RAINFOREST ANIMALS

The rainforest is home to many different types of animal.

Who lives here?

All kinds of animals, from elephants and tigers to bats, frogs and snakes, live in tropical rainforests. Many of the larger animals live on the forest floor, but lots of smaller animals live in the canopy. They use loud calls to communicate and move around by jumping, swinging or gliding through the trees. Spider monkeys, from South America, can use their tails to cling onto branches as they swing from tree to tree.

A spider monkey swings through the rainforest looking for food and shelter.

QUIZ TIME!

Which of these big cats doesn't live in the rainforest?

a. jaguar

b. cheetah

c. puma

Answer on page 32.

In temperate rainforests, in places such as North America, animals like wolves and grizzly bears live on the forest floor. Animals such as squirrels and chipmunks spend a lot of time in the trees, along with many types of birds.

Animal and plant partners

Plants and animals need each other. When animals such as monkeys, insects and birds feed on **nectar** in flowers, they pick up **pollen**, which they carry to the next flower. This pollinates the flowers so they produce fruits and seeds. Many other animals need to eat flowers, fruits and seeds to survive.

Plants also help animal life cycles. Rainwater held in bromeliads provides a place for poison dart frogs to keep their tadpoles safe.

Leaf-tailed geckos are camouflaged to look like tree bark.

Defences

Some animals use camouflage to hide from predators or prey. Sloths curl their bodies up to look like part of a tree as they hang upside down from a branch. Their hair is covered in green **algae** so they are well hidden among the trees. **Reptiles**, such as geckos, are hard to see because they look like dried leaves or moss. Chameleons can change to be the same colour as leaves or branches. Poison dart frogs have colourful bright markings to warn predators that they are poisonous. Tropical fish such as angelfish, which live in the warm waters of the River Amazon, often have striped bodies. Black stripes on a colourful background help the fish to camouflage themselves among the plants.

Poison dart frogs use the water that collects in bromeliads to keep their tadpoles safe.

? What other animals do you think live in the rainforest? Turn the page to find out.

Rainforest birds

Birds are important to the rainforest. When they eat berries and fruits, the seeds inside pass through their bodies and come out in their poo. This spreads the seeds around the forest where they can grow into new trees. Many different kinds of birds live in temperate rainforests, including pheasants, nuthatches and flycatchers. Colourful birds including parrots and toucans live in the tropical rainforest canopy. They have long beaks with sharp edges for tearing and crushing fruits and berries. Toucans and a type of parrot called a macaw nest in holes in trees. They live mainly in the canopy. Hawks, owls and eagles hunt for smaller birds and animal prey, such as reptiles, fish and **rodents**.

Toucans have huge beaks. Some beaks are nearly half as long as the toucan's body!

HAVE A GO

Scatter some mixed wild bird seed in the garden to see what grows. The plants that grow will produce more seed for birds to find and eat.

Quick FACTS

- All kinds of animals from frogs, birds and lizards to elephants and tigers live in rainforests.
- Some animals can also help to spread plant species around the rainforest.

QUIZ TIME!

Why do you think toucans have colourful beaks?

a. **to warn other animals they are poisonous**

b. **as camouflage from predators**

c. **to attract a mate**

Answer on page 32.

Make this

Rainforest rivers are home to lots of colourful fish such as the freshwater angelfish. Have a go making a shoal of these bright fish.

What other types of rainforest fish can you make? You could find out what they look like by using a book or the Internet.

1 Cut a paper plate into a simple fish-shape, like the one shown.

2 Paint the plate in a bright colour and leave it to dry.

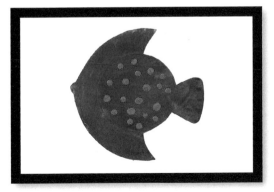

3 Paint colourful spots or scales on the body of your fish.

4 Use a felt-tip pen to draw thick stripes or other markings such as tail fins. Stick on a googly eye just above the mouth.

RAINFOREST PEOPLES

Tribal peoples have been living in the rainforests for thousands of years.

There are over a thousand different tribal peoples, mainly living in tropical rainforests around the world. Each tribe has its own way of life and language. They understand how important the rainforest is and care for it. They take only what they need for food, shelter and medicine so that they live in harmony with the trees or the animals that share the forest with them.

The Kayapo people live in the Amazon rainforest in Brazil.

QUIZ TIME!

Some rainforest peoples use poison from poison dart frogs for hunting.

Which of these is the most poisonous?

a. golden dart frog

b. strawberry poison dart frog

c. bumblebee poison dart frog

Answer on page 32.

Hunting and gathering

Rainforest peoples are skilled at hunting and tracking animals. They make their own hunting weapons such as spears for fishing and blowpipes that shoot poisonous darts. But they also use modern weapons, such as guns. They gather plants from the forest for food and medicine, but will also trade their goods with people from nearby towns and cities.

Yanomami hunters use spears, bows and blowpipes to hunt for their prey.

HAVE A GO
Try making a musical instrument using only natural materials, such as wood, bamboo, sticks, pebbles, nuts or coffee beans.

Rainforest children learn about forest foods and skills, such as hunting, from an early age.

Homes and communities

Some tribes move around the forest from place to place. Others live in one place and grow crops such as sweet potatoes. They use wood and plants from the forest to build their homes and make household items, crafts, hunting weapons and musical instruments. Some tribes live together in large homes around an area of land that they use for cooking, chores and ceremonies. In other tribes, men and women live apart. Children learn skills like hunting and tracking animals from their parents, families and other tribe members.

This Surui tribe member is wearing an elaborate tribal headdress made from feathers.

Under threat

Traditional ways of life of the rainforest peoples are under threat. In some places, outsiders have moved in and taken their land away. Some tribal peoples now only wear modern clothing and use modern tools and household items. New technology and contact with people from outside the forest can be good for tribal peoples, but their traditional skills and crafts could be lost if they give up the old ways of hunting, and living. Outsiders can also bring in new diseases that the rainforest people are not **immune** to.

Craftwork

Tribes have their own rich culture and art. Some tribes make craftwork to trade or sell to tourists. They are skilled at using materials including wood, plant fibres and feathers. Each tribe has its own way of making objects like masks and headdresses, which they also wear for dancing and ceremonies.

The Yanomami weave baskets - used for harvesting their crops - from strips of bark.

Make this

When tribal peoples celebrate their culture, they often wear amazing costumes, make-up and masks. You can make your own mask using card, paint, beads, feathers and scraps of fabric.

Perform a tribal rainforest dance wearing your mask. You could make a musical instrument to perform with, too

1 Cut an oval shape from cardboard that will cover your face. Cut holes for your eyes and nose and a slot for your mouth. (Ask an adult to help you do this.)

2 Cut out shapes from coloured paper and stick them onto the front of your mask.

3 Add spots, stripes and other decorations with paints or felt-tip pens. Leave your mask to dry.

4 Stick on strips of raffia for hair. Tape string decorated with beads and feathers to the bottom of your mask. Punch a hole in each side of the mask. Then tie elastic to the holes to keep the mask in place on your face.

SAVING RAINFORESTS

It is important to protect rainforests as many are under threat.

Large areas of rainforest are being lost every year as trees are cut down and an area is cleared, sometimes by setting fire to the trees. Some experts think that we are losing over 325 square kilometres of tropical rainforest every day. The forest is cleared to make way for logging, mining, cattle ranching or farming and new roads are built to move goods and people around.

Huge areas of this rainforest in Sumatra, Indonesia have been cleared by burning down the trees.

Climate change

Climate change is also a threat to rainforests. Scientists think that the Earth's climate is warming up because carbon dioxide and other **greenhouse gases** trap heat. These gases are produced by industry and transport and lots of **methane** is produced by cows! Trees store carbon dioxide in their wood and leaves. They turn it back into oxygen, which they release back into the atmosphere. Smaller rainforests means there are fewer trees making oxygen. When trees are chopped or burned down, the carbon dioxide inside them goes back into the atmosphere.

Logging companies cut down lots of tropical trees that are made into furniture and other goods.

Animals and plants

Some rainforest animals, such as elephants, orang-utans, jaguars and tigers, are **endangered**. This means they are at risk of dying out because of hunting, **poaching** and deforestation. Many other animals that live in the rainforest are also in danger. As more forest habitat is destroyed, we may lose as many as 50,000 plant, animal and insect species. In some forests, dams have been built across rivers to provide power for electricity for towns and cities. This can harm fish and other wildlife living in and along the rivers. Rainforest animals, including reptiles, big cats and birds are also taken illegally for the **exotic** pet trade.

Orang-utans are threatened by the loss of their rainforest habitat.

QUIZ TIME!

How many football pitch-sized areas of rainforest are cut down every year?

a. 1 million
b. 5.5 million
c. 8.5 million

Answer on page 32.

Quick *FACTS*
Threats to the rainforest and its animals are:
• Clearing trees for logging or farming.
• The exotic pet trade.

? Is there anything you can do to help save rainforests? Turn the page to find out.

Saving rainforests

What can you do?

We can all do something to help save the rainforests. We can try to raise money to help **conservation** organisations that work to protect the forests, their animals and peoples. We can find out more about rainforests and help other people understand

how important they are. We can look for things that are sold under the Rainforest Alliance (above, right) or Fairtrade labels, because they mean that the people who grew or made them have been paid a fair price for their work, and the land and rainforests have been protected, too.

Recycling paper

Another way we can help temperate rainforests is to make sure we don't waste paper. Many trees are cut down illegally every year to make paper. Using recycled paper and taking care not to waste paper helps to save trees.

HAVE A GO

Cut out designs from used gift-wrap or cards to make your own gift tags. Make a hole in the top of each tag with a hole-punch and thread ribbon or tape through it.

Make this

What other messages about rainforests could your T-shirt carry? You could make a 'save the tiger' or 'save the orang-utan' T-shirt instead.

You can help raise awareness about saving rainforests by decorating your own 'Save the Rainforest' T-shirt. You could make them for your friends and family, too.

1 Before you start, make sure you get permission to use a T-shirt. Draw the shape of a rainforest animal on card, such as a frog. Ask an adult to cut out the middle of the animal shape to create a stencil.

2 Tape a stencil onto your T-shirt.

3 Dab fabric paint through the stencil onto the T-shirt. Leave to dry. Repeat with the stencil in a different place or with another stencil.

HINT: if you flip your stencil over you will get a mirror image of your original image.

4 Paint the words 'Save the Rainforest' onto the front of your T-shirt using fabric paint. Leave your T-shirt to dry.

GLOSSARY

algae living things that are plant-like but have no leaves or roots

atmosphere a thin layer of gases covering a planet

bromeliads plants with a short stem and a rosette of stiff, shiny leaves

camouflage a way of hiding something so it looks like its surroundings

canopy something that forms a cover over an area

carbon dioxide a natural gas found in the atmosphere

carnivorous meat-eating

climate the usual weather conditions for a place

climate change the heating up or cooling down of Earth's atmosphere over a long period of time

conservation work done to protect and preserve

deciduous a type of tree or plant that loses its leaves each year

endangered an animal or plant that is in danger of dying out forever

Equator the imaginary line around the centre of the Earth

evergreen a type of tree or plant that keeps its leaves all year

exotic unusual or beautiful plants, animals or places

fungi a group of living things that includes mushrooms

greenhouse gases gases such as carbon dioxide that help trap heat in the Earth's atmosphere

habitat the natural home of an animal or plant

immune able to fight off a disease without medicine

mammals animals with hair that feed their young with the mother's milk

methane a natural gas

microbes tiny living things that can only be seen under a microscope

nectar sweet liquid that plants use to attract insects and birds

nutrients something in food that helps people, animals and plants live and grow

oxygen a natural gas found in the atmosphere

poaching illegally killing animals for their meat, fur, bones or ivory

polar the cold areas at the top and bottom of Earth

pollen tiny grains inside a flower that some plants use to reproduce

predators animals that hunt and eat other animals

prey animals that are hunted by other animals for food

recycle to break something down and turn it into something else

reproduce to make more of the same

reptiles a group of cold-blooded animals

rodents small mammals that have long front teeth

species a group of living things that share a name and can breed

spores tiny bodies that can grow into new plants

temperate a place with mild temperatures

tendril a thin shoot that plants use to help them cling onto things

tribal belonging to a group that shares the same ancestors, culture and beliefs

tropics the areas on Earth above and below the Equator

BOOKS

Eco Alert: Rainforests
by Rebecca Hunter (Franklin Watts , 2012)

Great Planet Earth: River Amazon
by Valerie Boden (Franklin Watts, 2014)

Espresso Ideas Box: Rainforests
by Deborah Chancellor (Franklin Watts, 2011)

Unstable Earth: What Happens if the Rainforests Disappear?
By Mary Colson (Wayland, 2014)

Up Close: Rainforest by Paul Harrison (Franklin Watts, 2011)

WEBSITES

www.kids.mongabay.com
A colourful website packed with facts on rainforests and the animals and peoples living in them.

www.msu.edu/user/urquhart/rainforest
The 'virtual rainforest' website, with pictures, videos, and lots of information about tropical rainforests.

www.rainforest-alliance.org/kids
The children's section of the website of the Rainforest Alliance, the organisation that runs a certification scheme for rainforest products, including facts, online games, activities and virtual rainforest visits.

NOTE TO PARENTS AND TEACHERS:
Every effort has been made by the Publishers to ensure that these websites are suitable for children, that they are of the highest educational value, and that they contain no inappropriate or offensive material. However, because of the nature of the Internet, it is impossible to guarantee that the contents of these sites will not be altered. We strongly advise that Internet access is supervised by a responsible adult.

INDEX

QUIZ ANSWERS

Page 4: a - the Amazon
Page 12: b - 45 metres
Page 18: b - cheetah
Page 20: c - to attract a mate
Page 22: a - golden dart frog
Page 27: c - 8.5 million